March On Children!

THE STORY OF JAMES MEREDITH'S MARCH AGAINST FEAR

WRITTEN BY: KATINA RANKIN

ILLUSTRATED BY: RESHONDA PERRYMAN

FOREWORD

I am overjoyed to write this foreword, not only because the author, my former student and mentee, happened to choose to write a children's book about my husband, but also because I believe in the need and value of Katina Rankin's mission to educate all children about a major and crucial era in America's developing republic. I also believe it is imperative that children learn of those courageous heroes, whether notable or unsung, who turned the pages of history from widespread overt and legal racism.

Upon meeting Ms. Rankin when she enrolled in the Graduate Communications Program at Jackson State University, I knew she would attain all her goals. A young, dynamic student, she quickly grasped the techniques of broadcast story-telling and how to communicate the information in an incredibly succinct and interesting manner to her audience. I remember how our television staff looked at each other as she wrote and delivered her first story with the confidence and personality of a pro. "The kid's got talent," our writing staffer exclaimed.

After many years as a TV news anchor, Ms. Rankin's amazing talents and skills are once again evolving in yet another genre. It is inspiring to witness her development as a children's book author while keeping intact her incredible attention to detail. Her stories are not only well written for young children, but they are absolutely factual, demonstrating her all-embracing knowledge of the book's subject.

Unlike other children's books that portray general information about a subject while using literary license to fictionally fill in the blanks, Ms. Rankin is committed to fact-based stories of those whom she writes about.

Ms. Rankin's book about James Meredith is right on point. In the 1960's, he was a loner, impassive by the Civil Rights Movement because he strongly believed the U.S. Constitution is all that is needed to guarantee his rights as a citizen. This wonderfully written book helps children to understand who James Meredith really is, and why, from an early age, he began a mission to change Mississippi and America into a better place for all citizens. Stylistically, her vivid storytelling, without a doubt, is a spellbinding experience for any child. I hope Ms. Rankin's book will be used by educators across the country as a viable tool to teach children in their early learning process the "truth" about James Meredith and why he believes the word "citizen" is the most important one in the U.S. Constitution.

Judy Alsobrooks Meredith, Ph.D

"Come on, Mom. I can't be late. I'm leading the march," Rankin yelled from the bottom of the stairs.

"I'll be down in a minute, Son," his mother Nan yelled back.

"What march?" Isabella asked Rankin.

"The March Against Fear," Rankin replied.

"What's there to be fearful of, and why are you leading a march?" Isabella asked.

"We're re-enacting James Meredith's March Against Fear," Rankin told Isabella.

"Who is James Meredith?" Isabella inquired.

"In his words, he is 'a bad man'," Rankin answered.

"Well, what did he do that was so bad?" Isabella asked her brother.

"He meant bad in a good way. You know like when we see a pretty girl and say she's bad," Rankin explained.

"He desegregated the University Of Mississippi or Ole Miss," Rankin told Isabella.

"Desegregated?" Isabella said. "You mean like the little girl, Ruby Bridges, who was the first black to go to that school in Louisiana?"

"Yes. But, James Meredith was a grown man. He was the first black man to enter the University of Mississippi. It was a big deal. President John F. Kennedy sent federal police to escort him to and from school."

"Why?" Isabella asked.

"As you know from reading about Mrs. Bridges, blacks and whites couldn't go to school together," Rankin explained. "People could get hurt trying to learn together. People were threatening Mr. Meredith's life if he went to that school. The police and military had to step in."

"Did they harm him?" Isabella asked inquisitively.

"Not at Ole Miss. However, they did when he led his March Against Fear," Rankin answered.

Mom walked down the stairs in a black pantsuit wearing a string of pearls. She grabbed her black clutch purse off the table and asked, "Are you two ready to go?"

"Yes ma'am," they answered.

On the ride to the school auditorium, Isabella said, "Are you going to tell me how Mr. Meredith got hurt in that march or not?"

"Watch the play, Isabella. You'll find out," Rankin told her.

"Isabella, do you remember when Rankin went to work with your Aunt Katina?" her mother asked.

"Yes ma'am," Isabella replied.

"Tee Tee Tina, as you all call her, is a journalist," her mother said.

"I know, Mom. She anchors and reports at the television station," Isabella blurted out.

"On one of those interviews, she took Rankin along with her and even let him ask civil rights icon James Meredith a few questions," her mother explained.

"I enjoyed talking to him so much and learning about his life that I asked my English teacher Mrs. Leftridge if we could do a play on his life. We narrowed down his civil rights works to a march he led," Rankin told Isabella.

When they made it to the school, their mother Nan straightened Rankin's shirt and brushed his hair. Nan said, "Break a leg" as Rankin headed backstage.

The lights in the auditorium went dark. A spotlight beamed on the red curtain displaying a white M on the material. The curtains slowly opened.

There stood Rankin on the left of the stage with students behind him. He began to walk and the students followed him. Rankin looked out into the crowd and recited these words by James Meredith, "If you don't remember anything else I tell you, remember finishing is far more important than starting."

"Why does that sign say 'Peabody' mom?" Isabella asked.

"Because that's where Mr. Meredith started his March Against Fear at the Peabody in Memphis, Tennessee.

He marched from Tennessee to Mississippi," her mother replied. "Shhhh, pay attention to your brother."

"I thought I was the baddest man that had ever been born," Rankin recited. "I was at war, and I thought I was gone win," Rankin said as he continued walking and sharing his story with other marchers across the stage.

"Were you afraid to step into the classroom at Ole Miss?" one of the marchers asked.

"I wasn't caring nothing about integrating nothing. My goal was to destroy the system of white supremacy," Rankin said in his Meredith role.

"To be courageous means there's got to be something to fear. But, I used a reverse psychology on fear," the young Meredith actor continued saying as they crossed the state line into Mississippi.

Kapow! Gunfire rang out when they made it to Hernando, Mississippi.

The young Meredith hit the ground landing on his stomach. A look of pain could be seen on his face. The marchers scattered. Meredith was shot by a White man named James Aubrey Norvell. Meredith was rushed to the hospital.

The curtain closed.

"Mommy, I asked Rankin if Mr. Meredith got hurt. He didn't tell me. He told me I had to watch the play. I guess that answers my question. But, I have another question. Did he die?" Isabella asked.

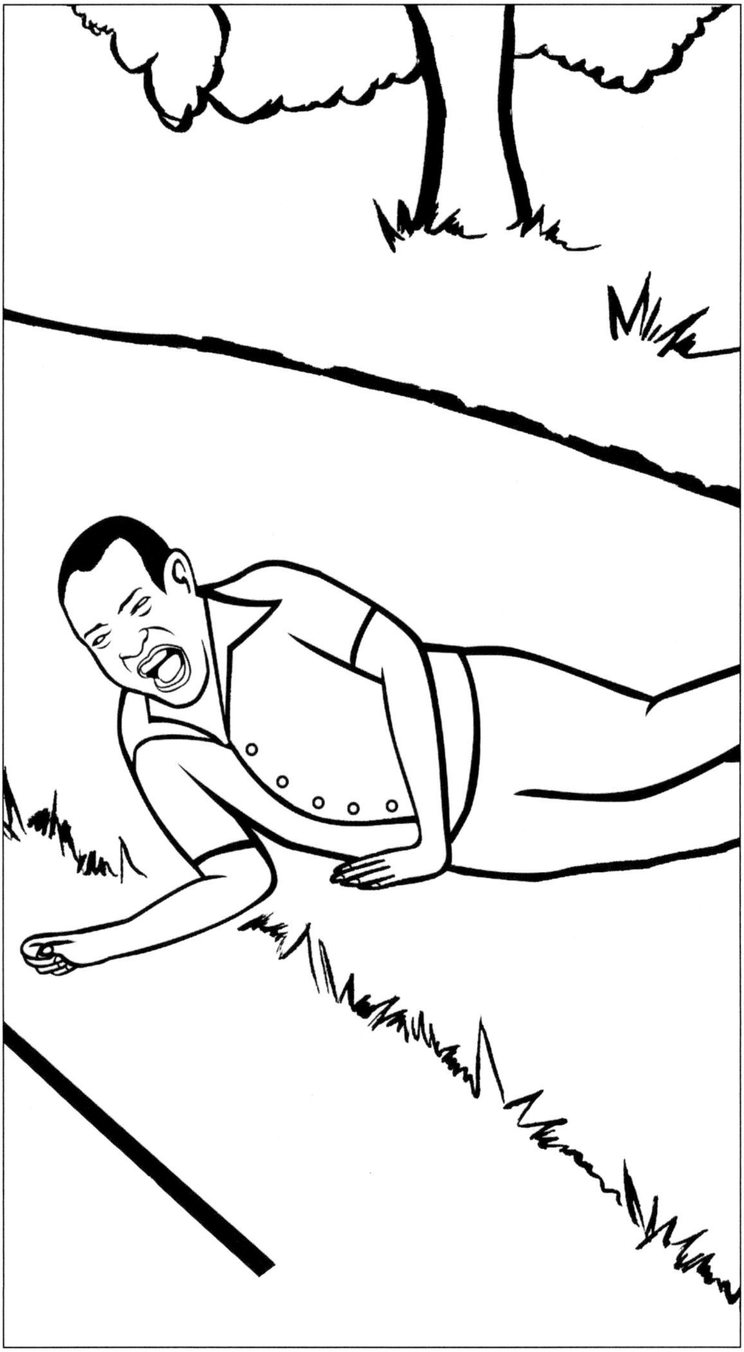

"You'll find out soon enough, Sweet Pea," her mother said as she put her arm around Isabella and gave her a hug.

The red curtains opened again.

"We must keep going," a marcher said.

"No way. We should give this up. Someone could have died and someone could die," another marcher chimed in.

"Yes. Think about it. This started out as a solo march. He didn't want this to be a media event," another marcher commented.

"Don't you remember what Mr. Meredith told us at the beginning of this March?" a third marcher said with authority. "Finishing is far more important than starting."

"Think about it. We can register people to vote if we keep going," another marcher remarked.

They placed one foot in front of the other. The march continued while James Meredith was hospitalized. Some big names joined the March Against Fear such as Dr. Martin Luther King, Jr. And, after a short hospital stay, Meredith rejoined the movement.

"Look, Mommy. Rankin's back. That means Mr. Meredith lived," Isabella blurted out.

"Yes, baby. Not so loud. Pay attention," her mother whispered.

"The two biggest problems in the world today is the black/white race issue and the rich/poor issue," said the young Rankin back in his Meredith role.

The marchers listened intently to Meredith as he kept talking and walking until 220 miles later when they reached the steps of the State Capitol of Mississippi.

Rankin slowly stepped in front of a podium and said, "When I talked to Mr. Meredith, he said these words to me. 'Am I or am I not a citizen?'

So I ask the same of you tonight. Look at the person next to you and realize we are all created equal. As we leave this auditorium putting one foot in front of the other, remember these words by Mr. Meredith, 'A walk is an exercise of the right of citizenship.' Today, will you begin your March Against Fear?"

The END

ABOUT THE AUTHOR

Katina Rankin, a native of Magee, Mississippi, is an Emmy-nominated journalist.

She received her bachelor's degree in mass communications from Alcorn State University and her master's degree in broadcast journalism from Jackson State University.

While attending ASU, Katina began her journalism career as an intern at WLBT. After six years on the air in Mississippi, Katina's career led her to Raleigh-Durham, North Carolina, where she co-anchored the main newscast at Eyewitness News.

During her journalism career, Katina has covered everything from the Mississippi murder trials of Byron De La Beckwith and Sam Bowers to the Space Shuttle Columbia disaster in Texas. She has featured local Miss America Pageant contestants by following them to Atlantic City, and she has traveled to San Antonio for the Final Four tournaments.

Katina's daily reports about the impact of Hurricane Katrina included an in-depth interview with Mississippi Governor Haley Barbour.

She also interviewed notable figures and broke many stories in the lacrosse rape investigation at Duke University in North Carolina.

Katina has also interviewed former NAACP president Myrlie Evers, presidential candidate John Edwards, the late Rosa Parks, the Reverend Jesse Jackson, the Reverend Al Sharpton, basketball greats Magic Johnson and Charles Barkley, and blues legend B.B. King. Katina also distinguished herself as a journalist by earning several news awards including an emmy nomination.

After more than seventeen years in broadcast and print media, Katina felt entrepreneurial, and she founded Katina Rankin Enterprises (KRE), a public relations firm. Katina's public relations work took her to three countries: Israel, Egypt, and Palestine. During her travels, Katina interviewed world peace advocate and recording artist Fred Nassiri and the Governess of Bethlehem, Palestine Salah Al-Ta'mari- just to name a few.

Katina's passion is helping people. She has given back to the community by speaking to hundreds of church groups, schools, and universities through the years. Katina believes proper training can help individuals realize their potential and help them get to the next level. Katina has taught writing classes at Jackson State University. Additionally, Katina has given the commencement address at Alcorn State University. And she has been featured on the Oprah Winfrey Show.

She is a member of Alpha Kappa Alpha Sorority, Inc., the National Academy of Television Arts and Sciences, the National Association of Black Journalists, and the Society of Children's Book Writers and Illustrators.

Katina has authored and published "Up North, Down South: City Folk Meet Country Folk," a children's book. The "Up North, Down South: City Folk Meet Country Folk" Coloring and Activity book was released in mid-December 2016. Katina's children's civil rights books: "Emmett Till: Sometimes Good Can Come Out of a Bad Situation" and "Medgar Evers: He Taught His Children To Crawl So We Could Stand" were published in the summer of 2018.

Katina has been named Mississippi's Woman of the Year and Shero of the Year for her work with women and children.

Made in the USA
Coppell, TX
25 January 2023

11689858R00026